#460

# THE SEA'S HARVEST
## The Story of Aquaculture

JOSEPH E. BROWN

# The Sea's Harvest
THE STORY OF AQUACULTURE

Illustrated with photographs and drawings

INTRODUCTION BY ROBERT B. ABEL,
NATIONAL SEA GRANT PROGRAM

DODD, MEAD & COMPANY · NEW YORK

FOR JOE AND ROSE

*Illustration Credits*

Australian Information Service, 12 (top left), 14, 25 (bottom), 52, 67; Australian News and Information Bureau, 12 (top right), 12 (bottom), 58; Joseph E. Brown, 74, 81, 82, 83; Bureau of Commercial Fisheries, 66, 68; California Department of Fish and Game 42 (top); Chemical Engineering, 19; Anne Ensign, 8, 91; Florida News Bureau, 24, 28; Fish and Wildlife Service, Department of the Interior, 57 (left); Japan Air Lines, 63, 64, 70, 79; Japan Trade Center, 11; Ocean Expo '75, 86; Oceanographic Commission of Washington, 16, 17, 21, 25 (top); Jack Schott, California Department of Fish and Game, 44; Charles H. Turner, California Department of Fish and Game, 40, 41, 42 (bottom), 53; Texas A & M University, 47, 48; U. S. Navy, 87, 88; Kate Urghart, Inmont Corporation, 57 (right), 60, 61.

Library of Congress Cataloging in Publication Data

Brown, Joseph E     1929-
   The sea's harvest.

   Includes index.
   SUMMARY: Describes the various projects involving planting, cultivating, and harvesting the many plant and animal resources of the sea.
   1. Mariculture—Juvenile literature. [1. Marine resources]   I. Title.
SH138.B76       639       75-9646
ISBN 0-396-07153-8

Copyright © 1975 by Joseph E. Brown
All rights reserved
No part of this book may be reproduced in any form without permission in writing from the publisher
Printed in the United States of America

# Introduction

For thousands of years, man has lived by the sea. He has sailed on it, fought on it, and died on it. Perhaps, then, it is an indication of the perverseness of man, that only since gaining the ability to leave his planet, has he evinced much interest in what goes on inside it.

This is especially true of the oceans. With the exceptions of the aquaculture practiced by the Chinese, Greeks, and Romans, described by Mr. Brown, oceanography—the study of the oceans—was almost an unknown science prior to a few decades ago. Now, thanks to several aggressive scientists and engineers, and enlightened governments, the oceans are receiving well-deserved attention.

This is particularly relevant to food. To the degree that man has used the oceans as a source of food, he has been primarily a hunter. In recent years, however, realizing that the seas are in danger of being "fished-out" by larger and increasingly sophisticated fishing fleets, oceanographers and biologists are attempting to turn hunters into farmers by introducing aquaculture to all coastal nations.

In the United States, in 1967 the Congress created the National Sea Grant Program to spur development of aquaculture (among other purposes). Sea Grant now sponsors nearly eighty projects to "farm" for lobsters, shrimp, clams, oysters, squid, and abalone, including nearly all of the domestic projects described by Mr. Brown.

But Sea Grant goes beyond "fish farming" in the strict sense. Interpreting the term more broadly, we also foster culture and harvesting of sea plant foods, the harvesting and processing of precious coral for jewelry, and discovery of medicines from organisms found in the deep ocean waters.

In pursuing such a mission, I am naturally delighted to introduce *The Sea's Harvest*. I hope that Mr. Brown will inspire thousands of young folks to greater understanding of our surrounding seas and appreciation for their practitioners.

ROBERT B. ABEL<br>
Director<br>
National Sea Grant Program

# Contents

|    | *Introduction*               | 5  |
|----|------------------------------|----|
| 1. | Why Farm the Sea?            | 9  |
| 2. | The Fish Farms               | 23 |
| 3. | Man Builds a Reef            | 38 |
| 4. | The Crustaceans              | 46 |
| 5. | Mollusks: The Shelled Crops  | 56 |
| 6. | Plants of the Sea            | 69 |
| 7. | Other Crops of the Ocean     | 76 |
| 8. | Tomorrow's Sea Farm          | 85 |
|    | *Index*                      | 95 |

*A representation of five commonly farmed crops of the sea. (Not to scale.) Bottom left: shrimp. Bottom right: oyster. Bottom center: lobster. Center: kelp (seaweed). Left and right, center: fish.*

*Chapter* **1**

# Why Farm the Sea?

For a long time after man began life on Earth, he sought the food he needed to survive by hunting and gathering. First with clubs and stones, later with bows and arrows, spears and other weapons, he roamed the forests in search of wild animals. He dug into the earth for edible roots. And from the meadows and valleys, he collected wild berries, fruits, and nuts.

Hunting and gathering occupied so much of man's time, in fact, that for thousands of years he remained a very primitive creature. Civilization—the forming of communities and the emergence of arts and crafts, the sciences and culture—did not really begin until early man made an important discovery.

By *farming* rather than hunting or gathering, he learned, a regular and ample food supply could be maintained with much less time and effort. By planting crops such as grains or vegetables in the spring, for instance, the harvest that followed in the fall would furnish food to last through the winter. By capturing and domesticating wild animals and then breeding them, humans could maintain an adequate supply of meat.

As man turned from hunting to farming, many changes

began to occur in his world. Individuals and families began joining into villages and communities. They shared the output of their farms and the knowledge of how their crops could be improved. With more time available, their civilization began to advance. This meant that instead of merely existing or surviving, they had time to devote to art and culture. In turn, these advancements led to a more pleasant and meaningful way of life.

The transition from hunting to farming occurred at different times in different parts of the world. It also occurred rather recently, when compared to man's time on earth. Although it is estimated that humans have existed from between 1 million and 5 million years, the first farms did not appear until a few thousand years ago. The period since then marks the advancement of the world's civilizations.

As he has gathered food from the land, man has also used the sea as a source of food. With nets, hooks, spears, and other weapons, he has for centuries "hunted" the animals of the ocean: fish; lobsters; oysters; whales, the largest of all animals on earth; as well as edible sea plants.

It was not until very recently, however, long after humans began farming the land, that they farmed the sea to any great extent. Farming in this sense does not mean random hunting, as in the case of commercial fishing from boats, but "planting," cultivating, and then harvesting the sea's various "crops" entirely in captivity, and under controlled conditions.

The science of land farming is called *agriculture*. We call sea farming *aquaculture*. It is sometimes also referred to as *maraculture*. *Aqua* is the Latin word meaning water, and *culture* means to cultivate.

Even more properly, the way we produce some kinds of seafood might be called ranching instead of farming. In true farming, everything is planted, cultivated, and har-

*A traditional form of hunting in the sea: a catch of mackerel arrives in port aboard a Japanese trawler, and is sorted for processing.*

*Cormorant birds are used by Japanese fishermen to assist in catching small fish. The birds snare fish underwater in their beaks, but cannot swallow them due to the lines around their necks.*

Left: An Australian trout farmer inspects some recently hatched fry. Right: A sample netting of eight-month-old rainbow trout farmed at a hatchery in Victoria, Australia.

Yearling brown trout are placed in an aircraft for lake planting in Victoria, Australia.

vested in one place. Ranches on the dry land, on the other hand, involve stocks of domesticated animals that are allowed to roam at large most of the time. Then they are rounded up by cowboys or ranchers and returned to captivity where they are prepared for market. In much the same way, sea "ranchers" in some parts of the world breed and raise fish in captivity, release them in natural waters, and later harvest them when they return to feed or spawn.

Whether by ranching or farming, the raising and harvesting of various seafoods is becoming an increasingly important source of food for the world. Combined with the hunting of fish, the oceans have always been a tremendous food supplier. It has been estimated, in fact, that sea resources, in a natural state, are probably *twice* as great as the earth's total agricultural food production.

Many factors have affected man's ability to farm the land and his reliance on food from that source. For one thing, the world population has been constantly increasing, and more people require additional food on which to subsist. At the same time, the increasing population means that more valuable land must be used for homes, factories, schools, and playgrounds. In turn this means that less land can be devoted to farming.

The seas, on the other hand, cover a much larger portion of the total earth, about two-thirds of its surface, in fact. In the last seventy years, the yield of seafood through commercial production has risen about fifteen times to a present average of 70 million tons per year, worldwide. Despite the oceans' vast yield, however, scientists have determined the approximate number of fish of any species that must be left alone or they will be threatened with extinction. Modern technology has reached the point where, by unlimited harvesting, the fishing industry would easily be able to take fish in numbers beyond this danger point. Already, there are

*An Australian trout farmer hauls in a load of trout to inspect their growth rate. Originally a freshwater species, these trout mature faster after being transferred to saltwater.*

species of fish and other marine animals so overfished that scientists fear it may be too late to save them.

Sea farming, then, seems a likely partial answer to this problem. In terms of annual production, though, it represents only a small part of all the food we receive from the sea. At present, sea farming around the world produces about 5 million tons of food annually, less than 8 per cent of all seafood. Of the 5 million tons, about 3.7 million tons —the majority—is fish. Another 1 million tons is harvested in oysters and other shellfish. Seaweed and other sea plants make up the balance of 300,000 tons of seafood each year cultivated by man.

Scientists estimate, however, that potentially the harvest of seafood can be increased to perhaps fourteen times the 5 million tons now produced. That would mean that sea farming would be almost equal to present-day sea hunting.

Generally speaking, more food can be produced in an area of comparable size in the sea than on "dry" farms. This is of course partly possible because in the sea, fish and other animals can be raised throughout the vertical water column, instead of only on a horizontal plane. The water column is how scientists refer to the entire volume of any portion of the sea, from the ocean floor to the surface.

Another reason is that many growing plants and animals multiply in the sea much faster than they do on land. In Japan, for instance, one company that is growing oysters has been able to harvest up to 50,000 pounds of these tasty marine animals from one acre of inshore ocean area. An acre of dry land planted in grass, on the other hand, grows only about 100 pounds of feed each season. And in Spain, where the growing of mussels is a specialty, sea farmers produce as much as 250,000 pounds of food from a single acre.

Although sea farming on a large scale is comparatively new, some forms of aquaculture have existed for thousands of years. The Japanese raised oysters as early as 2000 B.C. The Romans began growing them about 100 B.C. In Java, the raising of milkfish was such a large undertaking about 1400 A.D. that the theft of fish stocks became so common, laws were passed to punish the thieves.

Many of the same problems that ancient sea farmers faced still exist, and today some of the problems have increased. One of the major problems is high cost. Aquaculture involves farming the *edge* of the sea, not the deep part of it, and coastal land around the world is very valuable. In the United States, more than half the population lives within fifty miles of the coast. By 1980, this figure is expected to increase to about 80 per cent. As more people migrate toward the coast, the land there that they occupy

*Floating nets at Clam Bay, near Seattle, Washington, where coho salmon are being raised for market by Domsea Farms.*

becomes more expensive to purchase and maintain.

The edge of the sea offers far more than pleasure to people. It is also valuable in the sense that many industries—power plants, for example—can be operated efficiently there because inexpensive seawater is available for cooling machinery and they are also close to shipping terminals.

At the same time, the part of the ocean closest to the shore is the one that supports most life in the sea. This happens mainly because nutrients that sustain sea life empty into this region from the rivers tumbling down from inland mountains. Nutrients are various kinds of substances on which marine animals feed. It is for this reason that a considerable amount of the world's sea farming is practiced in estuaries, inlets, and bays.

Protected from the open ocean, these calm bodies of water offer a safe haven for young forms of marine life, many of which, after growing into adulthood, migrate toward the sea. Still later, they return to the estuaries and bays to spawn their own young, and the cycle of life begins once again.

Because of the high cost of land along the coast, it is becoming common for sea farmers to share the area they farm with another occupant. An example is a company named Domsea Farms, one of the newest salmon-farming projects in the United States.

To raise its fish for market, Domsea uses a part of the 235 acres owned by the U.S. Naval Supply Center at Puget Sound, near Seattle, Washington. The Navy does not require all of the land it owns there all of the time. Most of it had been used only as a storage area for petroleum used for naval warships, and as a storage area it is inactive. The own-

*Left: Young coho salmon are being prepared for transfer from creek to Clam Bay by Domsea Farms.*

*Below: Harvesting coho salmon by Domsea Farms at Clam Bay, Washington. Fish are sucked through tubular pump at left center, then sorted for size and quality.*

ers of the Domsea company worked out an agreement with the Navy to set out large nets on the Sound. Young salmon are placed in these nets and fed daily until they grow to adult size. Then, with smaller nets, the mature fish are harvested and prepared for market.

Because of the high cost of raising salmon, the Domsea company probably could not afford to operate if it had to pay the full rate for the water area it uses. By sharing the area with the U.S. Navy, however, that area is utilized to greater advantage by both occupants.

Another example of water-sharing is in Carlsbad, California, a small community thirty miles north of San Diego. There, the San Diego Gas & Electric Company operates a power plant which generates electricity for a large metropolitan area. As an experiment, a group of scientists from San Diego State University, under sponsorship of the Sea Grant Program, arranged to raise lobsters in the warm water discharged from the cooling unit of the plant. The lobsters were not the species normally found in California waters, however. They were *Homarus americanus,* or American lobsters, which normally live in waters off the New England coast.

By raising the lobsters in water higher in temperature than that normally found in the Carlsbad area, the scientists learned, the animals matured very rapidly. In fact, some grew to adulthood in only eighteen months, instead of the usual five to seven years.

Still a third example is found in the Gulf of Mexico, off the coast of Texas. Ever since rich deposits of oil were discovered below the sea floor of the Gulf many years ago, this body of water has been the site of intense oil activity. The oil is removed by drilling from huge platforms anchored to the sea floor.

Dr. Sammy Ray, a biologist on the staff of Texas A.&M.

*Oysters raised near a Texas power plant are inspected.*

University, discovered that oysters can be raised by using one of these platforms in partnership with the oil company that owns it.

Oysters develop rapidly from their initial larval stage into tiny *spats*, or seedlings. During their lives, they seek places in the sea onto which they fasten themselves. They feed on microscopic nutrients that drift past on the sea's currents. In his experiment, Dr. Ray developed a series of mesh bags in which he placed the young spats. The bags were not watertight; the spaces between the fibers were wide enough to allow water to flow through, but not so wide that the spats would be lost.

The oil platform was about twenty miles at sea from the city of Galveston, Texas. After carefully placing the young oysters in the mesh bags, Dr. Ray then lowered the bags into the water from the deck of the platform with a long rope line. There are strong currents around the platform, and these brought the nutrients that the young oysters required to grow. Because of the distance from the shoreline, Dr. Ray learned, the oysters were not damaged by the many forms of pollution that often harm oysters and other forms of marine life in inshore aquaculture areas.

The threat of pollution is the second major problem of sea farms around the world. As people continue to migrate toward the coastlines of their countries, the pollution increases. The same rivers that deliver life-sustaining nutrients to the estuaries and bays often also bring the residues of harmful pesticides and other toxic chemicals that man has developed from inland areas. Young forms of marine life are quite susceptible to these pollutants, no matter how small the quantity.

Most states in the United States, as well as other countries, now are aware of the danger of coastal pollution and have passed laws to prevent it. If aquaculture is to expand as a major form of providing food for the world, people must be constantly alert to the danger of pollution, and must be willing to enforce the laws designed to prevent it.

Considerable research has been conducted in recent years to determine just how various forms of pollution affect life in the sea. And research itself represents the third problem area in the new endeavor of aquaculture. For all the years that man has studied the sea, there is much about its forms of life about which he still knows very little.

In some countries, notably Japan, sea farming is mostly a commercial venture. That is, farmed seafood is grown almost entirely to feed people. This is necessary in a country like Japan which has a large population but a very small total land area, so little land, in fact that little is available for conventional farming, or agriculture. Long ago, the Japanese learned how to hunt and raise food in the sea at

*The product ready for market: coho salmon, Domsea Farms*

comparatively low cost, and the sea became a major source of Japan's food supply.

Many sea farms exist in Japan's Inland Sea, a large body of water that separates several of the country's islands. The raising of seaweed is a principal endeavor. Other farms are devoted to oysters, shrimp, and a shellfish called abalone.

In most countries, however, including the United States, aquaculture is still an experimental, research project. Scientists are still trying to find ways that seafood can be farmed in large quantities, and at a reasonable cost. The Domsea company mentioned earlier is an exception. Domsea is a profit-making company and it raises salmon for sale in stores and restaurants. But because of the high cost of raising these fish, they are still quite expensive when purchased in the stores, compared to many other low-cost food items originating on land farms.

In many universities throughout the United States, scientists are attempting to solve the various problems associated with aquaculture so that as the country's demand for food increases, food from the sea may become an important means of filling that demand. Then, commercial companies such as Domsea, which started with Sea Grant support, may be able to reduce their cost of operation and sell the seafood at prices the average person can afford.

What are the main problems facing the science researchers? One of them is the high mortality or death rate among young marine animals raised in captivity. One reason for this is the effect of pollution described earlier. But many of the deaths occur for reasons the scientists have not yet discovered.

This is why most American aquaculture projects, unlike those in Japan and a few other countries, are primarily experimental. Until a few years ago, these experiments were largely unconnected with each other. Since 1967, however, more than 120 American universities have been united in these efforts through a project called the National Sea Grant Program. Administered by the United States government, Sea Grant provides money to universities for research and development of many of the sea's resources, including food. Fisheries and aquaculture, in fact, collectively represent about one-fourth of the total Sea Grant effort. State agencies are also involved.

Since the program began, scientists have learned a lot about the problems of aquaculture in the United States. Using Sea Grant research, they have harvested the first commercial crop of cultured shrimp ever produced in the United States. They have determined, through engineering, how man can assist nature in bringing nutrients to the sea farms. And they have accumulated considerable knowledge on the kinds of marine animals that will grow best, with the least problems, in any given region of the sea.

Soon, perhaps in a few years, man will be able to put this knowledge to work on a large scale. He will do so as he expands his ability to farm the sea as he has for centuries farmed the land.

Chapter 2

# The Fish Farms

By far, the most abundant creatures in the sea are the fish. There are an estimated 40,000 species of fish altogether, counting both saltwater and freshwater varieties. They range in size from the tiny sardines, anchovies, and herrings to the large sharks, rays, and groupers. In spite of this large number, however, only a very few species are hunted by man, and even fewer are raised on sea farms.

Many of the species—the sharks, for instance—are not considered good to eat. There are others too tender to be caught commercially. They are easily bruised and damaged when hauled in nets or on hooks. Still other species are too few in number to be fished economically.

It is the task of the modern sea farmer and marine scientist, therefore, to attempt to determine the kinds of fish that can be most easily and economically grown by aquaculture techniques as a means of feeding great numbers of people.

In a number of research projects around the world, the aquaculturist is attempting to find fish that mature rapidly, are good to eat, are high in protein value, and are resistant to disease. In a very limited way, scientists have succeeded in what they call artificial selection, or artificial breeding. This is the creation of a new species of fish by crossbreeding

*A section of a Florida lake is netted off for an experimental project in raising catfish. Floats provide a platform for fish farmers to feed and harvest their crops.*

or other means. And in still another area of research, scientists are attempting to find uses for some fish which are considered worthless as food.

Unlike many creatures in the sea that do not migrate far during their lifetime—some of the sedentary shellfish such as abalones, for example—fish swim about constantly. Sometimes they migrate hundreds of miles each year. Pens of various sorts are therefore necessary in fish farming.

The simplest kind of pen consists of a mesh net placed across the mouth of a small bay or inlet. The flow of ocean water to and from the bay is not restricted by the net, and it is this flow, caused by the tides, that brings the food required by the fish.

In other aquaculture projects the pens are much more elaborate. Some of them involve large tanks containing seawater that are separated from the ocean, located perhaps dozens of miles from the coast. These are especially necessary in experiments in which young fish are raised from eggs. Even with the finest mesh nets, valuable eggs can be lost in estuary currents. Pollution and disease can also be more easily controlled in tank hatcheries.

An important part of all fish farming is feeding. Scientists must be sure that the fish will receive the right amount of food at the right time. Because the feeding process can be controlled and food is more readily available, fish raised in

*Left: Two kinds of pellet foods used by Domsea Farms to feed growing coho salmon.*

*Below: Three circular tanks, each with a 25,000-gallon capacity, where prawns are being raised in Australia*

captivity generally grow faster and are healthier than those competing in the wild state. Hunting for food requires energy, and fish use up a lot of the value of the food they eat merely in hunting for it.

So far, scientists have been able to grow only a few species of fish from eggs. One successful project was operated by the U. S. Bureau of Commercial Fisheries (now the National Marine Fisheries Service) at La Jolla, California. There, Pacific sardines and mackerel were raised from eggs to an advanced juvenile state. The mackerel grew to ten inches, and the sardines to about four inches. Both of these fish are so-called *bait fish*, meaning that they are caught by commercial fishermen to be used as bait in catching larger species. Others are caught to be processed into *fish meal*, either as a food supplement for humans or animals, or as a fertilizer.

At La Jolla, Dr. George Schumann, director of the experiment, fed the newly hatched mackerel and sardines bits of tiny plants and animals called plankton. As they grew in size, brine shrimp were added to the diet. Because of the regular feeding habits and the warm water added to the tanks, the fish doubled in size in just two weeks.

Scientists have learned that warming the water fish live in is a sure way of encouraging them to grow faster. Most species of fish grow very little during the cold winter months. The growth process is accelerated when the ocean water warms again in the spring. Scientists in Ardote, Scotland, proved this by raising fish behind two dams in a sea loch (lake). In the winter, warm water from a nuclear power station was released into the loch. The fish, members of the sole family, continued to grow through the winter at about the same rate as in the summer.

In Japan, fish farming is a large-scale industry. Aquaculture accounts for 6 per cent of that country's entire fishing industry, and Japan is second only to Peru in the amount of fish harvested each year. In one recent year, Japanese fish farming yielded 440,000 tons of fish, worth more than $277 million.

Depletion of coastal and freshwater areas in Japan, due to pollution, land development, and overfishing, has led Japanese aquaculturists to develop entire fish farms in manmade tanks away from the sea. There, Japanese scientists are attempting to breed new species of fish that someday will be hatched, raised, and harvested entirely in captivity.

One of the most popular sea-farmed fish in Japan is the *hamachi*. A member of the yellowtail family, the *hamachi* is only .14 inch long when hatched, but grows to a length of about 29 inches within only three years. There are about 1,300 *hamachi* farms in Japan. They are responsible for a harvest of nearly 40,000 tons of fish each year.

In the southeastern United States, one of the most popular fish selected for farming is the pompano. A medium-sized fish with spiny fins and a forked tail, the pompano is considered excellent eating and is fished commercially off the coast of Florida. Because it has a high market value, it has also been the subject of many aquaculture experiments.

So far, sea farmers have had difficulty raising pompano from eggs. In most experiments, instead, they gather newly hatched pompano in nets from tidal lagoons and estuaries and transfer these to tanks on land. Pompano are generally hardy fish. Although they have no teeth with which to defend themselves against predators, they eat a great variety of food and are less susceptible than many other species to changes in water temperature and its salinity or salt content.

One of the ways that marine scientists are attempting to stimulate the growth of fish is by injecting hormones into experimental species. The use of hormones to induce

*Youngster holds a catfish grown on an experimental fish farm in Florida.*

*Young catfish in the Florida project are netted so that their growth can be determined.*

spawning in fish was started in Brazil as far back as 1932. (Hormones are chemical substances found in parts of the body.) More recently, experiments with freshwater catfish in Oklahoma and Florida have proved quite successful and have encouraged scientists to try the same thing with saltwater species.

By injecting hormones, the reproduction rate of catfish in one experiment was increased 850 per cent—from 82,000 to 700,000 in a test group. Some spawned in sixteen to twenty hours after injection, and scientists hope that this method can increase fish stocks by enormous numbers. Select strains, they believe, will grow faster, be more resistant to disease, and less sensitive to negative influences in their environment.

In Hawaii, aquaculturists used an unusual method to encourage mullet to spawn on sea farms. The mullet is a member of a fish family characterized by silvery sides, a small mouth, and tiny teeth. They have been raised in captivity in the Orient for years. At first, scientists were unable to raise them from eggs and, like the pompano, they had to capture the young in the sea. At the Oceanic Institute in Hawaii, however, scientists were at last able to induce mullet to spawn in man-made environments. Mullet spawn only once a year, and the normal spawning period is from January to March. Scientists were able to net young mullet larvae for the experiment just after they had hatched in the sea, but all soon died. And since mullet spawn only once a year, the scientists would have to wait an entire year to begin again.

To overcome this delay, the Oceanic Institute devised a way, by using plastic sheets draped over the mullet ponds, to fool captive young fish into believing that the spawning period had arrived by October, and thus enable them to speed up the experiment.

The scientists had theorized correctly that the sunlight of the different seasons had a lot to do with telling the mullet what time of year it was. By changing the plastic sheets (which also proved useful in attracting algae on which the fish lived) the outside light could also be changed to create artificial seasons.

In 1971, mullet spawned for the first time in captivity in Hawaii. Scientists there are still studying the results, in the hope that mullet may become a large seafood industry in the Islands.

Altering the natural environment of fish by such means as plastic sheets is only one way that scientists are seeking ways of increasing fish production. Just as important is the process of artificial selection or artificial breeding mentioned earlier. This means that over a period of several generations of fish, scientists actually create new subspecies or hybrids by scientific means.

Artificial breeding has been accomplished with land animals and birds for a long time. Chickens are one example. The popular White Leghorn chicken, which lays between 100 and 200 eggs a year, is a descendant of a wild fowl in India that laid but 12 to 24 eggs in the same period. The same wild birds, which were not meaty enough to eat in the wild state, were also artificially bred to produce the domesticated Plymouth Rock and Rhode Island Red chickens, both popular species of frying or broiling chickens in the United States.

So far, only three fish in the world have been artificially improved with established and regular success. They are the trout, the salmon, and the carp.

Trout are among the most highly prized fish in the world as far as their food value is concerned. But they are generally a small fish, and to raise enough to market commercially is quite expensive.

At a New Jersey hatchery, scientists successfully increased both the length of these fish and the amount of edible meat on their bodies by careful crossbreeding among species. In a two-year period, they increased the trout's average length at maturity from ten to fourteen inches. In some experimental lots, the trout grew two or three times faster than those in other lots that were allowed to grow as they would in their natural environment.

Carp are perhaps the oldest domesticated fish in the world. Native to Japan, China, and Central Asia, they were introduced years ago to Europe and the United States. There are many species of carp, ranging in size up to twenty-two inches long. They are prized both as food and, because of their bright color, as decorative fish for aquariums.

Carp are found mainly in large rivers. In May and June, the females move into shallow water to spawn; they lay about 60,000 eggs each on leaves of water plants, then swim off to let their young hatch on their own. Carp are considered mature in three to four years, but they live considerably longer, perhaps longer than any fish on earth. A sixteenth-century Swiss naturalist named Gesner mentioned a carp 150 years old, and others are believed to have lived even longer.

On sea farms, mostly in Japan, scientists have crossbred many carp species to develop new strains with even brighter colors. One species, called *koi*, is prized very highly by the Japanese both for its food value and as decorative fish, and some are valued at hundreds of dollars each.

Other species that have been artificially crossbred with success include the salmon and, to a limited degree, the milkfish. Scientists find salmon particularly interesting to study because of their unique life cycle.

Hatched in inland freshwater streams, some of them dozens of miles from the ocean, the young salmon swim downstream as they mature, spending most of their lives in the open ocean. Just before it is time for the females to spawn, they return upstream once again to the very place where they were hatched. The instinct to do this is so strong that even dams made by man are no obstacle. In the Pacific Northwest, dam builders consider the migration so important that they have built "ladders" in the dams to assist the salmon in their homeward swim.

Shortly after spawning, the female salmon dies, and the newly hatched fish begin their own downstream migration to begin the life cycle once again. Because of their migratory habit, salmon are one species of fish that are actually "ranched" instead of "farmed."

In one experiment, researchers at the University of Washington in Seattle released salmon hatched in captivity into a fresh waterway that led to salty Puget Sound. In their natural environment, salmon are always hatched in freshwater, then migrate to the ocean, only to return four years later to spawn their young. The Washington scientists did not know whether the fish bred in captivity would do the same. Indeed they did, returning, not four years later but in three, to the same pond.

The family of milkfish includes a number of species closely related to the herring. They grow large at maturity, some of them to fifty pounds, and are marked by a deeply forked tail. Because their diet consists of plants instead of the tiny animals that many other fish eat, the problem of feeding them is not as great.

Milkfish are not considered a prime seafood in the United States. In the Pacific and Indian Ocean areas, however, they are widely harvested and eaten. It is for this reason that scientists are attempting to develop new, meatier, hardier strains of this species throughout this area. The value of milkfish as a sea-farmed crop is evident in statistics from the Philippines alone. There, more than 46 million pounds of milkfish are grown on sea farms and harvested each year, with a value exceeding $10 million.

Still another technique in fish farming familiar to the land farmer is that of transplanting. On many land farms, plants are raised from seeds under closely controlled conditions in greenhouses, then transplanted to open fields where nature takes over their care. To a limited degree, this also has been done in sea farming, involving both plants and animals.

One such successful animal experiment took place in England and involved a fish called the plaice. A member of the flatfish family, the plaice lives its adult life on flat, sandy ocean floors of the North Sea and along the coasts of England and France.

Plaice are harvested by trawlers and eaten by the millions each year in Europe. Yet despite their vast population, the number of plaice that survive from the time they are hatched until they are fully grown—about three feet long—is extremely small. It has been estimated, in fact, that only one in 100,000 fish manages to survive the three-year period to maturity.

In the early 1950s, Dr. James Shellbourne, a British biologist, decided to seek a way that young plaice could somehow be protected and raised in captivity during this critical period, and the high mortality rate reduced.

Shellbourne knew that plaice experience one of the most unusual biological changes of all creatures in the sea. Each adult female releases between 50,000 and 70,000 eggs during her first spawning. The eggs, however, are not only tiny—about 1/12-inch long—but are also very buoyant. During the three weeks required for the eggs to hatch, these eggs, floating on the surface, are scooped up in huge numbers by birds and other predators.

Even after hatching, the young plaice remains near the surface. At this stage, it is shaped more like a tiny tadpole than a fish, and is about the size of a quarter. Then a curious process known as *metamorphosis* begins. Each day for about seven weeks, the tadpole shape changes slightly, until the shape is that of a flatfish. At the same time, the left eye of the young plaice moves slowly to the right side of the body until it finally resembles a true flatfish, like its relative the halibut. Only then does the plaice lose its buoyancy and sink to the bottom where it enjoys greater protection from predators.

In a series of experiments conducted during the 1950s, Dr. Shellbourne attempted to raise plaice in a laboratory tank at Port Erin, England. First, he collected eggs at sea in nets, then transported these to his fish farm. At the farm, he was able to control pollution with chemicals, and he attempted to keep the water temperature the same as that in the North Sea where the plaice had originated.

Even with these precautions only a single larva of the first 1,000 Shellbourne attempted to hatch survived. He was not disappointed, however, and by 1958—seven years after the experiment began—he had increased the survival rate to 6 per cent.

Dr. Shellbourne found that the cost of raising plaice on his sea farm far exceeded their value on the market. He estimated that it cost about sixty cents a pound to raise these fish that would sell for only thirty cents a pound. By continuing the unique experiment, Dr. Shellbourne and his colleagues hope to increase the rate of survival and decrease the cost at the same time. If their work succeeds, plaice could become an important sea-farmed product in England and, at the same time, reduce the cost and inherent dangers of fishing for this species in the harsh North Sea.

Each year, British fishermen alone catch about 45 million plaice in the North Sea. If each of a comparable number of fish raised in captivity required one square foot of bottom space, that same number could be grown in a shallow pond covering only 1¼ square miles. In addition, Dr. Shellbourne has suggested, if the pond were located near a power plant whose discharge would warm the water, growth would be greatly speeded. It is this kind of bold experiment, repeated in research projects around the world, that gives the sea farmers hope that aquaculture someday soon may become an important supplement to fish hunted by more traditional methods.

Still other research is directed at finding ways that fish considered useless as food may be put to a useful purpose. One is a method for processing fish flour, called either fish protein concentrate (FPC), or marine protein concentrate (MPC). This concentrate is a tasteless, odorless, stabilized powder made from whole fish by removing water and oil.

The value of FPC (or MPC) is its content of protein, an essential in the diet of all animals, including man. Perhaps surprisingly, five out of every six people on earth are vegetarians. This means that their diet consists mostly or entirely of plants, and thus they are denied important enriching substances found in fish, fowl, or meat. By processing fish flour, however, scientists are seeking a way that the less nutritious diets can be supplemented with FPC and their body-building values enhanced.

A major advantage of FPC is that it can be stored, shipped, and distributed throughout the world at normal temperatures. Transporting meat, poultry, or fish requires refrigeration and other precautions.

The concept of FPC is not new. The Romans created a substance from small fish that they called *liquamen*. Pliny, a Roman historian, pointed out in his writings that the fish used to produce liquamen were otherwise useless and undesirable. Biscuits were made from fish flour in the nineteenth century, but it was not until 1968 that any serious attempt was made to process FPC in the United States.

In that year, an experimental plant was built at New Bedford, Massachusetts, which later produced twenty tons of FPC daily from 100,000 pounds of fish. In this process, however, the odor of fish was not removed and the FPC was used only for feeding animals. This plant has since been closed.

Still later, in 1970, the National Marine Fisheries Service established another experimental plant, at Aberdeen, Washington. Opened a year later, it produced fifty tons of FPC daily from hake, an abundant species of fish found in both the Pacific and Atlantic.

Measuring twenty inches long and weighing two pounds at maturity, hake were considered worthless until recently because their skin is easily damaged in capture. The Russians, however, have used hake as food for many years; up to 85 per cent of this fish is valuable protein.

Marine scientists estimate that hake off the coasts of Oregon and Washington alone amount to one to two billion pounds, so there should be an abundant supply of this fish for FPC processing for many years.

The Aberdeen plant was purely an experimental venture. After three years of operation, it was closed down while government scientists studied the results. Most of them concluded that, while it had been proven that an odorless FPC product could be developed from hake, the process itself is quite expensive and ways must be found to reduce the cost.

So far, research projects in sea farming have ranged from complete failure to moderate success at best. In some parts of the world, domestic raising and harvesting of fish is a profitable venture, but this occurs only in areas where fish is such an important and vital part of the diet that people are willing to pay the costs involved in processing it.

In their comparatively recent research, scientists have established that two major factors affect man's dream of being able to farm the sea as well and wisely as he has farmed the land.

One is the need for strictly enforcing commercial fishing regulations so that the open sea will not be overfished. The decline and near-disappearance of some species of fish in the oceans has resulted from overfishing. When any species of animal in the sea is taken in enormous numbers and its population reduced, the important marine food chain is affected.

In the food chain, the larger but less numerous feed upon the smaller organisms. Greater quantities of food are required on the lower "links" of the chain to sustain the few but larger animals and birds near the top. Anything that influences the marine food chain in the open sea can also affect what is grown on sea farms, too.

The second factor is pollution. Especially in the estuaries, where the rivers meet the sea, control of pollution is vitally important. Although there are now laws in every coastal state to regulate fish-killing pollutants, fish still die by the millions each year along our coasts. The damage is multiplied many times if it occurs during the spawning season. Although minor pollutants may kill only a few fish in any area, if those fish are females that are about to spawn several thousand eggs, the loss multiplies tremendously.

And if that happens, hungry humans will be denied much of the potentially valuable crops that the sea offers in great quantities.

*Chapter* **3**

# Man Builds a Reef

Badly battered by a hurricane, the cement-hulled freighter *Sapona* broke her moorings one day in 1926 and sank slowly to the bottom of the sea near the island of Bimini in the Atlantic. The *Sapona* was an old ship, hastily built to serve in World War I. Because it was not of much value, her owners decided it would cost too much to salvage the vessel, and it was abandoned.

Soon, curious things began to happen as the *Sapona* lay on the sea bottom. Within days, green algae began to form on her broken cement hull. Attracted by this algae, which provided them food, schools of tiny fish began appearing where none had been before. Larger fish moved in to feed upon the smaller ones. Within only a few weeks, in an area that had been barren of marine life, a teeming community had been created.

How did this happen? Very simply, the sunken freighter had become an artificial reef.

It is well known to marine scientists that wherever natural reefs exist the likelihood of communities of marine organisms is greater than in barren areas of the sea. Coral reefs, living organisms themselves, are a good example. The greatest abundance and variety of fish and other marine creatures are found in the tropic and subtropic areas of the world noted for their coral reefs.

For the same reason, objects placed in the sea by man also become reefs. Since oil was discovered in the Gulf of Mexico, for instance, dozens of drilling platforms there have attracted huge communities of marine life around them. The pilings of piers and wharves perform the same function.

Years after the *Sapona* sank, the site remains a popular spot for diving-spearfishermen and marine scientists. The spearfishermen are attracted by the rich hunting grounds, the scientists by their desire to study a man-made reef. Unlike most ships whose hulls are made of steel, the cement construction material of the *Sapona* will never rust or rot away. Thus it is likely to be a gathering place for marine creatures for centuries to come.

The *Sapona*'s sinking was of course an accident. The oil platforms and wharves and piers were built for other purposes. But for several years marine scientists have been purposely sinking all sorts of objects in various places around the world to create artificial reefs. They are hoping to find the kinds of materials that will attract the most fish and other forms of life. These reefs represent another way in which man is attempting to help nature in producing food for his own needs.

The secret of a reef as a fish producer is a natural phenomenon that scientists call *stereotropism*. This is but one form of *tropism* in nature, in which plants or animals are attracted to or repelled by response to an external stimulus. On land, the turning of the sunflower constantly toward the sun or another light source is an example of tropism.

In the case of a reef, this compulsion begins with the smallest forms of life, the algae, that gather first on a new, hard object in the sea. After algae are established, increasingly larger forms of life, each feeding on the smaller one that preceded it, arrive.

Old car bodies are dumped to form an artificial reef off the California shore.

In the United States, experiments with various kinds of artificial reefs date back as far as 1931. In that year, the state of New Jersey became the first of twelve coastal states to provide funds for reef experiments. The project was a brief one, and the results somewhat disappointing. Although fish were indeed attracted to man-made objects placed off the New Jersey coast, the project itself was too limited to determine if large-scale building of artificial reefs could return a profit to commercial or sports fishermen.

Experiments since the thirties have been more encouraging. From 1947-1954, for instance, the Hawaii Fish and Game Division, under the supervision of Michio Takata, conducted a series of reef experiments on three barren ocean areas near the island of Oahu. Takata collected several scrapped used-car bodies and dumped these into the sea. Later, he added specially built concrete structures. In both cases, fish populations around the man-made reefs multiplied enormously, and within a very short period of time.

Scrapped automobile bodies were also used in a project begun off the California coast in 1958. It was sponsored by the California Department of Fish and Game. Hauled aboard a barge into Paradise Cove, near Los Angeles, twenty car bodies were dumped at the site. A few days previously, a team of divers had determined that very little

*A school of pile surf perch swim about an artificial reef in a California experiment.*

Worn-out street cars are prepared for dumping into the sea to be used as artificial reefs.

Human passengers once rode on the seats of a street car that these braces supported. Now the seats have become an artificial reef home for a sheephead.

marine life existed there naturally. Only hours after the last air bubbles ceased rising from the car bodies, the divers returned. This time they could hardly believe their eyes. Now, the site teemed with life: schools of surf perch and sargo, followed a little later by kelp bass and small California halibut.

Daily, as the divers revisited the area, the fish population continued to increase. Sheepshead, opaleye, sand bass, and rockfish soon joined the earlier arrivals. And by October—six months after the car bodies were dumped—small stands of kelp, known to provide excellent hiding places and food for fish, began flourishing as well.

Results of the Paradise Cove experiment encouraged California marine biologists to extend their investigation elsewhere along the coastline. Instead of car bodies, however, they next tried six wooden streetcars that had been scrapped. They were placed ten feet apart in water sixty feet deep near the community of Palos Verdes.

Led by biologist-diver John G. Carlisle, a diving team had first surveyed the site, and found little marine life. Only a few bottom-dwelling invertebrates, eleven Pacific sand dabs, and one electric ray were seen. A month later, the fish community had expanded so rapidly that an unexpected problem arose. Hundreds of divers and spearfishermen had learned about the "fishing hole." They came to the site in such great numbers that measures had to be taken to protect the marine life the reef had attracted.

Similar experiments have followed in the United States. In one of them, scientists are using television as a means of monitoring how various species of marine life react to a reef constructed of concrete blocks placed in a depth of forty-five feet of water off the coast of San Diego, California. Scientists of the sponsoring Scripps Institution of Oceanography placed a television camera on the sea bottom so that

*Wooden structures make excellent artificial reefs but often do not last long. Teredo borers made short work of this four by four inch timber placed in the sea off the California coast.*

they could watch the reef twenty-four hours a day. At a small public museum operated by Scripps, there is a second television receiver where visitors may watch, too.

Enterprising Japanese scientists have attempted to form reefs by dumping rocks into the sea. Their research has become so advanced they have developed two different kinds of reefs. Each is created for a special purpose.

The first kind, called the *tsukiiso*, is a low-lying reef built in shallow water. It is used mainly to promote the growth of various kinds of seaweed, harvested in great quantities in Japan.

The second is a reef the Japanese call the *gyosho*. Built in much deeper water, it attracts populations of fish and invertebrates, including the sea cucumber, sea urchin, and spiny crayfish.

In the Inland Sea near Kagawa Prefecture, Japanese

marine scientists built one of the largest artificial reefs in the world. It is literally a fish "apartment house," made from fifty reinforced concrete blocks with walls four feet thick and openings in each side. From previous underwater studies of the kinds of terrain various marine animals prefer, the Japanese are continuing to experiment with the underwater apartment. They are confident they will soon determine what kinds of materials work best in the sea to build reefs for specific animals.

In much the same way, American marine biologists feel that such "apartments" may be an ideal way to protect the population of lobsters. This is particularly true off the coast of Maine where lobster fishing is a large industry. Biologists there have warned that continued capture of these animals in large numbers may drastically reduce their population.

Most promising, they feel, would be apartments built of cement blocks near areas where discharge from coastal power plants warms the water. Lobsters would be attracted to the area by the cement blocks which would provide them with places to hide from predators.

Warmed by the power plant discharge, they would grow faster. If the experiments now under way prove successful, it would also show that the power plants themselves need not be potential sources of marine pollution, but valuable aids in farming the sea.

*Chapter* **4**

# The Crustaceans

Within the broad phylum of marine creatures we call the *arthropods*, there is a class of shelled animals which includes a few species that have been sea farmed around the world.

They are the shrimps, lobsters, and crabs, all members of the class Crustacea of the Animal Kingdom. Crustaceans are the sea's shelled swimmers and crawlers. Unlike mollusks that grow by adding material to the edge of their shells throughout their lives, crustaceans shed their shells from year to year in a process called *molting*. Crustaceans are also considerably more active than the sedentary mollusks, crawling or swimming about freely in the sea.

In a very general way, we might describe crustaceans as water-breathing "insects," since the classes of Crustacea and Insecta are probably descendants of a common ancestor. There are about 25,000 species of crustaceans altogether.

Crustaceans are characterized by their jointed legs and hard shells. Most are adept at performing work tasks (and defending themselves against predators) with pincers or claws, which also places them ahead of mollusks in an evolutionary way. These "armored hands" are also used by the crustaceans for gathering and cutting their food.

The shrimp is unquestionably the most popular species

*A flume drain (lower right) has been found to be the most efficient method of harvesting shrimp raised by a Texas A. & M. scientific team. As water is pumped through the drain, a net catches most of the crop.*

of crustacean with the sea farmer, both because of its high food value and the fact that it grows to maturity in only a year or so. In both Japan and the United States, commercial shrimp harvesting is a multimillion-dollar business. Shrimp is the leading seafood industry in the Gulf of Mexico, where millions of these little shelled swimmers are harvested by colorful fleets of trawlers. Americans alone eat an estimated 400 million pounds of shrimp every year, over half of which is imported.

Delicate in flavor, they command high prices on the market. They are prepared either as the main course in a meal, or as an appetizer. In Louisiana, shrimp are a main ingredient in a popular, thick soupy dish called *gumbo*. In Japan, large numbers are harvested for preparation as *tempura*, a form of fried shrimp.

*Top Left: Shrimp moving to harvest at Corpus Christi, Texas, are hand-helped into the harvest flume.*

*Right: Harvesting of shrimp in a Texas A. & M. University project is by means of a large drain pipe and net. As water in the pond is drained, the net fills with shrimp.*

*Left: Sea-farmed shrimp harvest close-up*

Shrimp vary widely in size. The smallest, called the brine shrimp, grows to only about the size of a small pea, and is gathered mainly as food for other marine animals. The common pink shrimp, on the other hand, grows to eleven inches or more and, along with the white shrimp, brown shrimp, and Caribbean brown shrimp, is the most commonly sea farmed of the crustaceans.

Farming of shrimp has been carried out on a primitive scale for many years in Asian countries, particularly India, Indonesia, the Philippines, and Japan. The general practice in these countries for a long time was to remove young shrimp from the sea and place them in tanks for fattening up for market.

In the early 1950s, a Japanese scientist, Dr. Motosaku Fujinaga, thought that it was possible to raise shrimp entirely in captivity—from spawning to harvest. A determined man, he retired from a job with the Japanese government to devote full time to proving his theory.

Choosing the wheel shrimp for his experiment (because of its large size: nine inches at maturity), Dr. Fujinaga collected a number of adult females from commercial trawlers. One such female will lay about one-half million eggs. Dr. Fujinaga soon learned, however, that the females must be quickly separated from the eggs or they will devour them. By careful experimentation, Dr. Fujinaga determined the conditions that eventually led to successful breeding, care, and harvesting of his shrimp. His early work helped set the stage for shrimp farming in other countries of the world, including the United States.

Eggs, once laid, must be agitated by compressed air, and natural conditions of the sea must be closely simulated. The water temperature must be maintained between 77° F. and 84° F. by means of heaters. The salinity of the water must be just right. If these conditions are met, the shrimp larvae hatch from the eggs in about thirteen to fourteen days.

The larvae are self-sufficient for only about thirty-six hours, then amounts of microscopic food must be introduced. At the beginning this consists of tiny diatoms, or microscopic plant plankton. Later, the young shrimp are fed a meat diet consisting of copepods, brine shrimp, or oyster eggs.

Next, after the shrimp are old enough to gather their own food, they are transferred to rearing ponds. These ponds are quite shallow, and their bottoms are covered with sand to provide a hiding place for the shrimp during the day.

Considerable circulation of the water is required for the shrimp to survive. In Japan, Dr. Fujinaga developed ways to harness the movement of the tides for this purpose, thus saving the expense of costly pumps and other equipment.

In the United States, the first major harvest of sea-farmed shrimp did not occur until 1972. This was the result of a project that began five years earlier, in 1967, when a commercial company called Marifarm was launched at Panama City, Florida, on a 2,500-acre tract of land and water.

Unlike Dr. Fujinaga's project, Marifarm did not breed its shrimp in captivity. Instead, the company hired regular shrimp boats to capture female shrimp that had spawned in deeper waters off the Gulf of Mexico, and were about to lay their eggs. These were rushed to thirty-six hatching tanks, then were cared for in much the same manner that Dr. Fujinaga found feasible in Japan.

Like the Japanese, Marifarm found that extreme care is required in raising shrimp, or their mortality rate will be high. Scuba divers were employed to regularly inspect the extremely fine mesh nylon net that was designed to keep the shrimp in the rearing ponds, and the predators out.

Temperature during growth was critical. So was the necessity of lowering the temperature just before harvest so that the metabolism rate of the mature shrimp would slow down and they would not perish during transportation to market.

Raising shrimp for bait or to sell to oceanariums and aquariums as fish food involves somewhat less effort. This is because these shrimp—tiny brine shrimp primarily—are both small and hardy. Brine shrimp rarely grow bigger than five-eighths of an inch long, and they are almost transparent. Because there is such a large market for them as fish food, an increasing number of sea farms are devoting themselves to raising them in the United States.

A company named Calimar, Inc., which operates a brine shrimp facility in California's San Diego Bay, is typical. The company has leased six large tidal lagoons from another company which extracts salt from the bay. No pens are necessary; the brine shrimp naturally cluster in the area. To harvest them, skiffs and nets are used to skim the shrimp from the surface. Taken ashore, they are washed in freshwater tanks, then frozen for shipment across the country. Calimar harvests about 1,000 pounds daily in the summer, and 100 pounds daily in the winter.

Mexico is another country that is beginning to sea farm shrimp on a large scale. In 1972, the Mexican government announced a plan to establish a network of shrimp farms in coastal lagoons. Research to determine the best species of shrimp to raise was begun at the same time at the Monterrey Institute of Technology in Guaymas, on the west coast of Mexico.

Mexico is an ideal country for shrimp farming. Its coasts contain many inlets and lagoons, just the kind of ideal protected areas necessary for raising these tasty marine animals. And shrimp is a major seafood industry in Mexico, where 1,000 shrimp boats harvest an estimated $33 million

*Two fisheries technologists work in the laboratory of a freshwater lobster farm near Lancelin, Western Australia. Sponsors of the project hope to eventually market 500,000 pounds of this species each year.*

worth of shrimp each year in the Gulf of Mexico and the Gulf of California.

To a lesser degree, the lobster is being studied as a possible crop for sea farming. Unlike shrimp, little is known about the life cycle of the lobster even in its natural habitat. Scientists still do not know exactly how long it lives, the size of its population, its migratory habits, or all the predators that affect it.

In their natural environment, lobsters have been considered an important seafood for centuries. Long before the Pilgrims landed in America, Indian women waded into the cold surf off the coast of present-day New England to gather them for food. Much later, when scuba diving became so popular in the mid-twentieth century, lobsters became a choice item for underwater hunters.

Commercially, lobsters are captured in cratelike traps, called *pots*. These are placed on the sea floor and their location marked on the surface with buoys. Pieces of tempting food—sections of fish, crabs, even parts of other lobsters—

are placed in these pots as bait. Fishermen then visit their traps by boat, pulling them to the surface and removing the lobsters caught inside.

Unlike the shrimp, lobsters require a long time to mature—up to six years for some species. Raising them therefore is quite expensive.

One method of sea farming lobsters has been to rear them under controlled conditions, then release them into the open sea along the coastline at spawning time. It is not known, however, how successful this method has been in expanding the lobster population, since it is impossible to tell the difference between a lobster hatched in captivity and one born in the sea. With other species of marine animals, such as fish, scientists can plot migrations and biological activity by *tagging* their specimens—fastening a small metal tag on released animals. Like the shrimp, the lobster sheds its shell each year and a tag would thus be lost.

In most respects, the lobster's life cycle is like that of the shrimp, although both habits and physical characteristics of the lobster vary widely from species to species.

*Spiny lobsters on a rockpile near the California coast. This species does not have the large claws that characterize the East Coast lobster.*

In the United States, for example, there is one major biological difference between lobsters found on the New England coast and those that inhabit West Coast and southeastern waters. The American lobster has large claws. The West Coast species or spiny lobster (in the Southeast they are usually referred to as rock lobsters) does not.

Although many attempts have been made to raise lobsters on sea farms, most have failed, mainly because of the lack of knowledge about these shelled animals. In very recent years, however, marine biologists have compiled considerable new information from which more successful progress has been made.

In the Southern California project mentioned briefly in the first chapter, scientists are enthusiastic that American lobsters may soon be grown in commercial quantities.

Using the warm thermal discharge water of a San Diego coastal power plant, they have managed to duplicate the environmental conditions of the New England coast. The young lobsters, kept in plastic trays and tanks, range in size from one-quarter inch to three pounds. They live in a mixture of intake and discharge water drawn from a lagoon near the power plant. Water temperature can be very closely controlled.

The researchers have encountered several problems. One is the fact that lobsters constantly fight among themselves, often killing and eating each other. They must therefore be carefully watched and separated when this occurs. It is also difficult to maintain *brood stock*—mature adults from which new generations of young will be hatched. Maintaining an adequate supply of low-cost food is yet another concern.

In a project at the University of California campus at Davis, Dr. Robert Schlesser is specifically studying the problem of cannibalism—the destruction of lobsters by their own kind. By trial and error, scientists have made great strides toward this and other problems. They are hopeful that within a few years, lobsters will be added to the increasing list of crops man is farming regularly in the sea.

Crabs are caught commercially in enormous numbers each year in many countries of the world. As yet, they offer only a potential to the sea farmers, and very little experimentation has been done with them in captivity.

The largest of the commercially harvested crabs is the king crab of Alaska. It often measures five feet across its shell and weighs up to twenty-five pounds. Other popular seafood species are the rock crab and blue crab. Like lobsters, they are caught mostly in traps, or pots, which commercial crabmen bait and set out along the coastal sea floor. Frozen herring has been found to be the best bait.

The long time required by crabs to reach maturity is one reason they are not extensively farmed. Scientists recently have been studying ways that one unique biological feature of the crab may one day help overcome this.

Like many crustaceans, crabs grow new limbs—or claws —whenever an existing one is lost. This process is called *regeneration*. With most crab species, it is the meat inside the claws, not that in the main body, that provides the best food for man.

If studies can determine how fast this regeneration takes place, and whether it can be speeded up by artificial means, it may be possible to harvest only the claws from year to year. Shorn of this succulent part of its body (which apparently is a painless process) the crab would then continue to grow new ones. In this way, the crab would continue to produce a seafood crop throughout its lifetime without being killed itself, much as does the sheep its wool, the cow its milk, and the chicken its eggs.

*Chapter* **5**

# Mollusks: The Shelled Crops

The ancient Romans and Japanese were probably the world's first sea farmers. Their crop—the oyster—remains today as one of the most abundant marine animals cultivated by man. In the United States alone, farmed oysters account for more than half of the nation's annual harvest of this delicacy of the sea.

Together with clams, mussels, and scallops, oysters are the major edible member of the phylum of mollusks, *Mollusca*, one of the oldest and largest groups of sea animals with more than 100,000 known species.

Oysters and their mollusk cousins are characterized mainly by their shell, having either a single side or two sides hinged together by a thick muscle. (Not all mollusks are shelled, though; the octopus, for instance, is also a member of this family.)

Oysters, which have two shells, are a choice seafood and are high in food value. Sometimes they are eaten raw, served in the same shell that housed them throughout their life. They can also be stewed or cooked in various other ways.

Bivalve (two-shell) oysters are popular sea-farmed animals for many reasons. For one thing, they bring a high

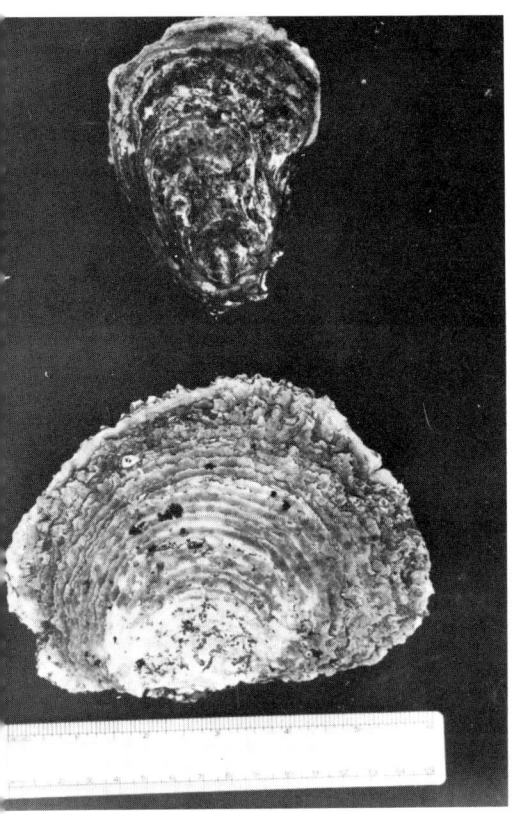

*Left: A comparison of two species of oysters: the American oyster (top), and the European oyster (bottom). Right: Close-up of an American oyster.*

price on the seafood market because of their demand. They grow fairly rapidly, the rate depending upon water temperature and other factors. And, perhaps most important, they do not move about during their lifetime, so fences or pens are not required.

The life cycle of the oyster is a fascinating one. The female oyster releases between 15 million and 115 million tiny eggs in a single spawning, usually during the warm summer. These eggs hatch into free-swimming larvae called *veligers*. The act of spawning has been described as an explosion, because of the tremendous number of eggs released; observers can see a large white cloud of larvae form almost instantly.

For two or three weeks, these veligers drift about in the currents, looking for a solid, clean surface upon which they eventually attach themselves. Sometimes the objects on which they fasten themselves are the shells of other, dead oysters. For this reason, the law in some states requires that shells of harvested oysters be returned to the sea so that baby oysters can attach to them.

On sea farms, man has provided a number of artificial surfaces for oysters to grow on. In some experiments, columns of cement discs, or parts of old oyster shells, are suspended on wires from floating rafts. The advantage of the column system is that the vertical depth of the farm area can be used to advantage, and more oysters can be grown per acre than if they were grown only on the bottom.

Suspending oysters also keeps them out of reach of bottom-crawling predators. One American oyster producer found that by "hanging cultivation," up to 64,000 pounds of oysters could be harvested from a single acre—many

*Picking up a load of matured oysters from a sea farm in Australia*

times that possible on the bottom only.

Oysters attach themselves by means of a tiny foot. At this stage they are called *spats*, the word originating long ago when fishermen thought the adult oyster "spat" out its eggs during spawning.

Only now, after it has settled on a flat surface where it will remain for life, does the young oyster begin to feed regularly. It does this by filtering tiny particles from the water through a series of latticelike gills, and catching them on hairlike stalks that surround the gills. It is believed that an oyster can filter two or three gallons of water each hour in this manner.

By filter feeding, the oyster risks one of the many dangers that have accounted for heavy losses of its population both in nature and on sea farms. This danger is silting, when mud or other debris flowing through the filter system becomes too thick and jams. For this reason, farmed oysters are often moved from place to place where silting, or the danger of pollution, is less. In a Florida research project, marine scientists found that by dumping huge piles of old oyster shells on the sea floor to form artificial reefs, oysters grew far enough off the bottom that silting was no longer a problem.

There are many animal predators of the oyster, the major one being the oyster drill. As its name implies, this tiny pest literally drills its way through the oyster shell to reach the oyster meat on which it then feeds. Marine scientists have found, however, that various chemicals can be distributed in the water of oyster farms to control the drill, but not kill the oyster. Likewise, quicklime can be used to kill predatory starfish which also feed on growing oysters.

Oyster farmers have learned there are several ways to reduce the time required for an oyster to reach maturity. The water temperature is an important factor. In Long Is-

*Starfish, predator of the oyster*

land Sound, for instance, it takes four or five years for oysters to reach market size, while in the Gulf of Mexico, which is much warmer, they mature in about half that time.

Oysters grow more slowly in colder water because in shutting their shells to protect themselves against the cold, they reduce the amount of water filtered and thus the food intake. For this reason, many sea farmers are attempting to warm the water artificially, such as using the warm water discharge of power plants.

A century ago, New Yorkers spent almost as much money for oysters as they did for meat. Oysters were at that time a $50 million-a-year business in New York. But overharvesting, pollution, and natural predators reduced the industry's worth to about $1 million a year. Not long ago, an experimental breeding laboratory and a sheltered nursery were established on Long Island, utilizing the discharge of a municipal power plant. Oysters there now mature at the same rate they do in the Gulf of Mexico—about 2 to 2½

A diver brings a dredge full of oysters, raised near a Long Island power plant, up for harvest.

A biologist checks growth of oysters in a Long Island project.

years. And within a few years, it is hoped, the Long Island industry will again be at a $50 million-a-year level.

Scientists have not yet definitely established whether warm water discharge from power plants, often referred to as thermal pollution, is harmful to other marine species.

Abundant supplies of "seed" oysters are required to maintain crops of these animals on sea farms. One common method begins with selecting mature adult oysters on the basis of shape, size, and growth. These are placed in tanks in which the water temperature is maintained at 50° F. for a short time. Then, the temperature is slowly raised over a period of about a month to 77° F., at which time spawning occurs.

The eggs are then transferred to rearing tanks. Algae—microscopic marine animals and plants—are introduced into the tanks as a source of food. As the larvae grow, the amount of algae is increased.

About two weeks later, the larvae are ready to attach themselves to a solid surface, just as they would in a natural habitat. Sea farmers assist them in this process by placing solid objects in the tank. Sometimes this consists of oyster shells carefully scrubbed to prevent harmful bacteria. The shells are in turn placed in still another tank while the transformation of the oyster from larva to spat takes place. In this step the oysters are kept in mesh bags.

About a week later, the bags are transported to open ponds where they are suspended into the water from the surface. Nutrients are carried through the mesh to the filter-feeding oysters, yet predators, such as starfish, cannot get through.

Although this method of culturing oysters can be more closely controlled than by simply suspending solid objects in the water and waiting for larvae to arrive, it is far more expensive. But, increasingly, sea farmers have been willing to invest larger sums of money because stocks of naturally grown oysters have declined in many parts of the world. Overfishing of natural stocks, one of the major causes, is not new. On the coast of Great Britain, for instance, huge mounds of oyster shells harvested centuries ago indicate the great numbers that were taken. In one place on the coast of Brittany, there is a single mound 15 yards high, 700 yards long, and 300 yards wide. It contains not only oyster shells, but those of scallops, clams, and mussels as well.

The problem of pollution in bays, inlets, and estuaries is also of major concern to biologists as well as oyster aquaculturists. It is also of concern to the farmer of the oyster raised not for its meat but for its valuable pearl.

There are two main types of pearl oyster: the Asian species, farmed mostly in Japan, and the Margarita oyster, raised in the southern Caribbean Sea off the coast of Venezuela.

*Oyster farms in a sheltered lagoon in Japan*

In Japan, where the pearl oyster is called the "tear of the moon," oyster farming accounts for 95 per cent of the world's cultured pearls. And although other types of manmade gems have reduced the artificial pearl market somewhat, pearls are still an important business there.

Pearl oysters are grown and harvested much the same as those grown for their meat. There is one important additional step, however. When the oyster is young, a tiny foreign substance is inserted into its shells. It is this minute irritant that the growing oyster covers with a secretion that forms the pearl.

Natural pearls are formed the same way, except that nature provides the irritant in the form of a pebble or other foreign matter passed along with nutrients.

Pearl harvesting is a colorful ritual in Japan, particularly in coastal villages such as Toba where the entire ecomony

*Pearl-harvesting* ama *girls in Japan. The large wooden barrels, which float, are towed by the girls and used to store the pearl oysters they harvest.*

depends upon this industry. When mature, these oysters are gathered by woman divers called *amas*. They dive to thirty feet or more in the sea, where the oysters lie on the bottom. Through long training, *amas* are able to remain submerged for several minutes, while they pry loose the mature oysters. Returning the the surface, the *amas* then place the oysters in wooden buckets which are hauled aboard boats for sorting and processing.

Harvesting meat oysters is usually done by dredges. These are scooplike metal nets that are dragged along the sea floor by boats. Oysters missed by the drag are hand-plucked at low tide, so that the bed may be cleaned and reseeded.

So far, no one has found a way of removing the meat of the oyster from the shell by machinery. This is done entirely by hand, and since many oysters are needed for a single gallon of meat, oyster shucking is a skilled trade and one requiring great dexterity.

Once the meat is deftly scooped from the shell, it is sorted on a table according to grade and size. Then it is packed under refrigeration for transport to market. Since oysters lose their flavor very quickly, time is essential in the transition of the oyster from its undersea bed to the dinner table.

Although clams, mussels, and scallops belong to the same family, they are not considered as choice a food as the oyster, and the industry farming them is likewise smaller.

Unlike oysters, clams move about slowly during their lifetime. They are hatched from larvae spawned in huge numbers, just like the oyster, but instead of attaching themselves to a hard surface, they burrow into the soft sand where they may remain for as long as twenty-five years if they are not dug up.

Clams vary widely from species to species, and the spe-

*A surf clam, a species gathered but not yet extensively sea farmed*

cific type determines its popularity as a food item. Soft-shelled clams, for instance are in great demand for the popular clambake, long a favorite activity particularly along the New England coast. Clams called long necks or steamers are the main ingredient in clam chowder, a thick, tasty, and very popular souplike dish.

Clams are harvested either by hand, or by using a clam dredge. A rake is used in hand-harvesting. It is dragged through the soft sand at low tide, scraping the clams to the surface. This is slow work, of course, and the process can be speeded up by using the dredge.

A sort of moving ramp, the dredge is mounted on the side of a boat. A hose attached to the bottom of the dredge, just above the clam beds, shoots a stream of water into the bottom silt, loosening the clams, rocks, and other items buried underneath. A conveyor belt brings all of this to the surface, where the clams are separated by hand.

Although mussels are very high in important protein, vitamins, and iron, they are only a minor sea-farmed crop in the United States. But in parts of Spain, Holland, France, and Italy, they are raised in great quantities. They are grown from seeds either on flat bottoms or suspended on strings, very much like oysters. Part of this mussel harvest is used by canneries, while other mussels are sold as fresh meat in markets of western Europe.

The scallop is a minor source of food throughout the world, too, except on the coasts of America. Of major interest to marine scientists are the many habits that differentiate it from other bivalve mollusks. Unlike the oyster and the mussel, for instance, the scallop not only swims quite freely, but it swims both backward and forward. It does this by opening and closing its two shells so that jets of water squirt out rapidly and provide propulsion.

There are about 300 species of scallops, and they reproduce and feed much as other bivalve mollusks do. The scallop is distinguished from the others by its system of more than 100 tiny blue eyes that are lined up just inside the lips of its shells. Scientists are fascinated by the similarity of the structure of these eyes to those of human beings.

*A marine biologist and his assistant examine the progress of mussels grown from rafts in an experimental project in New South Wales, Australia.*

*Scallop—an Alaskan weathervane scallop with a lemon for size comparison*

Though the scallop cannot see as well as the human, its eyes help it detect the presence of predators, such as the starfish.

In medieval times, the scallop was adopted as a symbol of courage and chivalry, as well as being harvested for food. Its shell was worn as a badge by knights, and its design was copied as a feature of heraldry on many fabrics. Historians suggest that this esteem of the lowly scallop probably resulted from a peculiar militarylike maneuver for which it is noted. Swimming together in great numbers, scallops are often remindful of fleets of miniature navies, sailing through the bountiful sea.

*Chapter* **6**

# Plants of the Sea

So far, the sea-farm crops we have discussed have consisted entirely of animals. There are plants in the sea, too, and although they differ in many ways from most plants on the land, they are extensively farmed in the ocean, particularly along the coasts of the continents where they grow in the greatest abundance.

Most sea plants are members of the Algae family. More commonly, they are called seaweeds. They range in size from minute plant plankton, that sometimes discolor the water along the coast, to the giant kelps. The largest and fastest growing plants anywhere on earth, kelps often grow 120 feet tall. Seaweeds are as varied in color as they are in size. Some are blue-green, others are entirely green, and still others are red or brown. The entire Algae family numbers about 15,000 species and they are found mainly in the tidal area just off the coast, or on the seashore itself.

Although many seaweeds are commercially valuable, it is only in Japan, China, and the Pacific islands that they are farmed extensively for food. In most other areas of the world they are harvested for fertilizer, as a base for medicines and pharmaceuticals, or for use in various industrial

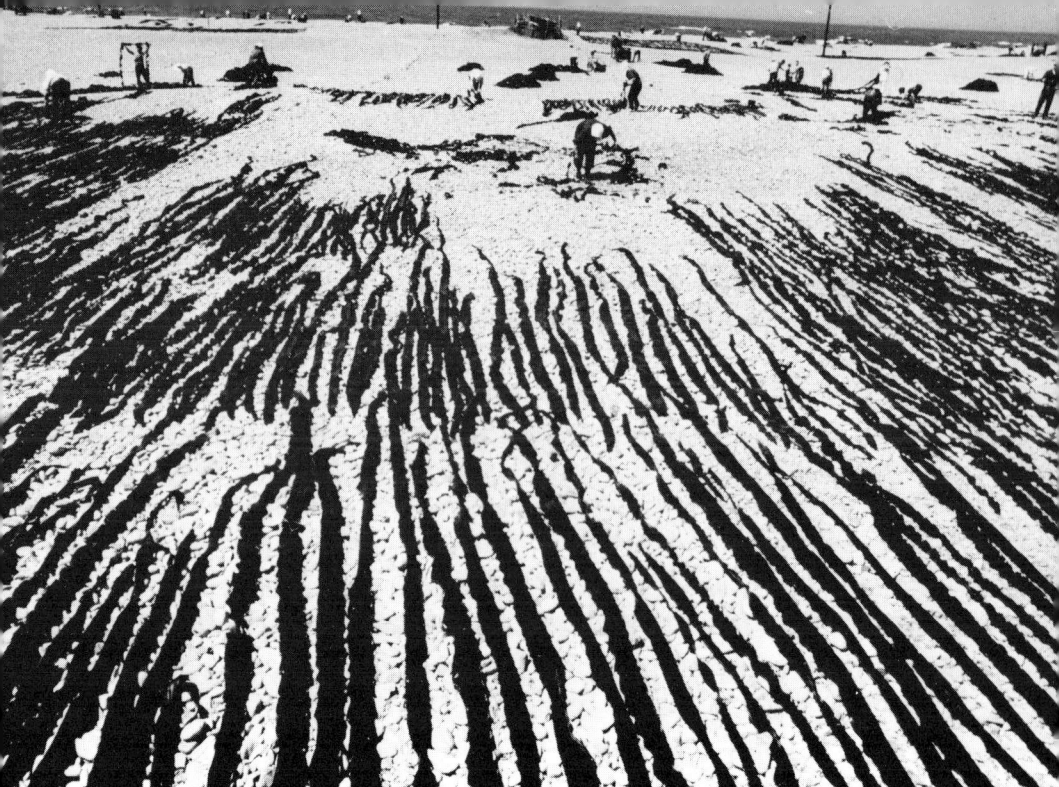

*Sea-farmed seaweed drying in Japan*

products. In Australia, there is a large industry devoted to extracting sodium alginate from seaweed to be used in frozen or dehydrated food processing. And on the West Coast of the United States, the harvesting of fast-growing kelp is a multimillion-dollar industry. An extract called *algin*, which is used as a thickening agent in jellies and a number of other products, is the principal use of this kelp.

The farming of seaweed dates back many centuries. Many early peoples used it for medicinal purposes and as a food delicacy. Extensive farming on a large scale, however, was not undertaken until about the mid-seventeenth century in Tokyo Bay, Japan. There, enterprising Japanese sea farmers began cultivating a species of seaweed they called *nori* or *amanari*. From that beginning, Japanese algae farming has increased in size to an industry employing one-half million people and covering thousands of water acres.

Small quantities of *nori* are eaten fresh. Most of it is sun-dried before being marketed. To grow *nori*, the Japanese select a small inlet or bay which is protected from heavy surf. There are several ways that cultivation is achieved. In one method, bamboo poles are driven in shallow water into the ocean floor and mesh nets strung between them, parallel to the surface. The nets must be deep enough so as not to be uncovered at low tide, but shallow enough so that the seaweed that grows on them can be hand-picked at harvest time.

Japanese sea farmers "seed" their wet *nori* fields in September or October when the water temperature drops and the mature plants are ready to produce *spores*, or seeds, that will in turn produce young plants. The spores drift through the water for a day or so, then settle on the netting and bamboo poles to which they fasten themselves.

Except for marine grasses that are not true algae, seaweeds do not have roots. They fasten themselves to solid submerged objects by means of gripping stems called *holdfasts*. These prevent them from being pushed away by currents. They receive their nourishment through *photosynthesis*. This is the scientist's name for a process by which plants convert energy received from sunlight into nourishing substances.

After harvesting, *nori* must be washed thoroughly to remove sand and mud. The leafy fronds are then chopped fine and spread on small bamboo mats to dry in the open air. After drying, sheets of *nori* are stripped from the mats, pressed, and prepared for market.

Different grades of *nori* are determined by the purity of the plant. The final product is used in soups, sauces, sandwiches, macaroni, and various other commodities.

*Nori*, like most seaweeds, is very high in food value. It

contains more than fifty times the amount of vitamin A found in an equivalent amount of chicken eggs. An algae relative, *dulse*, contains 25 per cent protein, 44 per cent carbohydrates, and 27 per cent mineral salts, making it a very nutritious plant indeed.

In Hawaii, various species of seaweeds have been used as food since ancient times. The most diversified use of seaweed as a dietary supplement was developed during the nineteenth century, where seventy-five different kinds were used regularly for food. In most cases the algae, which the Hawaiians called *limu*, were chopped up and used as a relish in combination with nuts, fish, octopus, squid, and other foods.

Each *limu* had a special use. Some, harvested in very small quantities, were considered delicacies of nobility; in fact, they were grown only in royal gardens.

Dulse and Irish moss, other algae, are used as food in parts of western Europe, the maritime provinces of Canada, and New England. Dulse is eaten raw, cooked with soups, eaten with fish and butter, and used in a variety of other ways.

Irish moss is dried and eaten out-of-hand like popcorn, or it is used in making soft jellies. The jelling qualities of Irish moss are due to a colloidal material, called *carrageenan*, found within its cells. A soft jelly bread is also made from this plant.

Irish moss derives its name from the country of Ireland, where it was first harvested. Early American colonists imported large quantities to make favorite desserts. In 1835, colonists in Massachusetts farmed huge beds of Irish moss, and it accounted for a booming industry in the community of Scituate in that state. Even today, nearly 10 million pounds are being processed yearly in New England and the Canadian Maritimes.

Irish moss is usually gathered by raking from small boats or from the shore. It is scraped from the rocks by long-handled rakes, but only the uppermost, large blades are removed, so that the plants underneath will continue to grow. If the bed is properly raked, more than one crop can be harvested during the season, from May to September. Although mechanical harvesters have been tested, none yet has been found to be as effective as the hand method.

Mechanical harvesters have been used for years, however, in mowing and collecting the upper fronds of giant kelp which grows in great abundance along the west coast of North America.

Survivors of the Ice Age, these brownish plants grow in beds one or two miles square off the western coast and they have become an important marine resource. There are about 1,000 species of giant brown kelps altogether, and most grow beyond the surfline on the coasts.

The largest species, *Macrocystis pyrifera*, is harvested by barges operated by several companies. Various animal feeds and a chemical called algin are the principal products. In California, where giant kelp beds are perhaps the thickest, strict regulation by the California Fish and Game Commission governs the harvesting procedure.

Only mature beds are cut. At the time of harvest, the kelp plants are dense on the surface with a high percentage of mature fronds present. These, for the most part, are about to die. Many are already dead. If left alone, these fronds would fall off and break loose from the parent plant to rot in the water or drift upon the nearby beach to cause litter.

Cutting removes the dense mat of material on the surface. Light then can penetrate to reach the immature fronds and this in turn accelerates their growth. Observations made by divers indicate that plants cut back in this

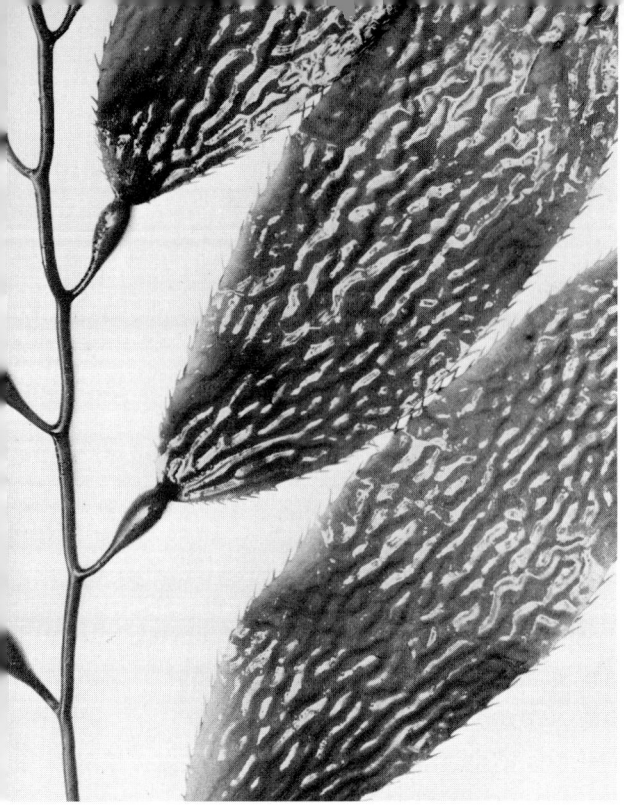

*Close-up of fronds of giant kelp*

way will grow new leafy stipes (or stems) twenty feet long within a few weeks.

Kelps traditionally have been among the sea's crops that have been collected or gathered, but, except for a few countries, not planted and cultivated. In 1974, two institutions announced plans to construct a series of kelp farms off the California coast. The sponsors of the project, which will take several years to complete, are the Sea Grant Program and California Institute of Technology.

Scientists at the two institutions knew that although kelp is a fast-growing plant, its range is sharply limited by water depth, temperature, bottom terrain, and seasonal storm conditions. Kelp grows best in water 20 to 80 feet deep, and it will not thrive at all in water much deeper than 130 feet.

The scientists, working in cooperation with the Naval Undersea Center, hope to increase the extent of the California kelp beds by creating "artificial bottoms" for them. They chose as a site a seven-acre area near the north end of San Clemente Island, twenty miles off the coast of Los Angeles. There, they installed a horizontal network of plastic ropes up to two inches in diameter at a depth of 40 feet in water 300 feet deep. The net was anchored to weights on the ocean floor.

Early in the project, 100 mature kelp plants were transplanted from their natural habitat to the new kelp farm. Scuba divers were used to tie the *holdfast* of each plant to the rope network. (Holdfast is the term for the lower part of the kelp plant that fastens itself to the bottom for security.)

Dr. Howard A. Wilcox, a physicist managing the project, described the project, actually begun with Sea Grant support in 1968, as "the world's first marine energy farm." The energy he referred to is, first of all, that generated by sunlight which is necessary for kelps to grow. But it also means future possible uses of kelp in addition to its present role in food and industrial products. "If we can grow these plants in sufficient quantities," he explained, "they might provide us with a vast amount of petroleumlike products for generating not only food, but fuels and electric power." The experiments will continue for many years, and they could eventually expand to include kelp farms 100 miles square.

About 60 per cent of the kelp harvested at San Clemente would be used in experiments to produce synthetic natural gas, methane. Another 30 per cent would be used to make fertilizers and plastics. The final 10 per cent would be processed as fodder for sea urchins, fish, and abalone kept in shoreline pens or tanks. All three of these marine animals have been sea farmed to produce food for humans.

Thus, for the first time on a major scale, man could be generating energy, harvesting food, and producing industrial products—all from the same farms in the sea.

*Chapter* 7

# Other Crops of the Ocean

Scattered through the seas of the world are billions of tons of small plants and animals called *plankton*. Most of them too small for the human eye to see, they drift about lazily with the currents, providing a basic food for many larger animals.

Plankton have been described as the equivalent of the grasses that grow on the dry land continents, and the comparison is an appropriate one. In potential food value, however, plankton far outweigh that of the land grasses. One scientist has estimated that while grasses of the world produce about 40 billion tons of valuable carbohydrates each year, the sea's plankton generate more than twice as much.

Despite their enormous food potential, little effort was made until recently to farm plankton as we farm grasses on land. Now, marine scientists have at last begun to study the possibility, especially as the sea's resources loom even more important as a means of feeding an expanding world population.

Probably the first major interest in plankton as a food occurred during World War II. Since military leaders knew that plankton was a possible source of food for hungry airmen or seamen lost at sea, they devised simple plankton scoop nets which they then placed in survival kits.

No one yet has seriously suggested that "plankton-burgers" may soon become popular around the world. As a possible farmed supplementary food source, however, plankton is gaining considerable interest among marine scientists.

One type of plankton that seems to have great harvest possibilities is a tiny shrimplike creature called *krill*. Growing to two or three inches long, krill provides the major food for the giant blue whale, the largest animal ever to inhabit the earth. Realizing that this whale may grow to 100 feet and weigh 150 tons at maturity, it is not surprising that each one devours more than one ton of krill daily.

Krill swim about just below the surface in huge schools sometimes miles wide, mainly in the cold Antarctic. Because of their pink color, they often appear as a solid reddish mass when viewed from a ship or from the air.

Krill are very high in food value. A pound of these crustaceans contains about 460 calories—about the same as shrimp or lobster to which they are related.

If the krill can feed such huge creatures as whales, many scientists reason, they must certainly be contenders as a new food source for man. In Russia, scientists conducted experiments that showed that krill can be caught in large numbers quite easily and processed to produce animal food.

One Russian ship, the trawler S.S. *Knipovitch*, has reported catches of up to six tons for half-hour trawls. Krill harvesters have reported one major problem, however. If the shells of the krill are not removed immediately after they are caught, the meat decays rapidly. Facing this concern, Russian scientists have begun looking for an inexpensive method to mechanically de-shell krill aboard ship.

One innovative Russian scientist has designed a large submarine which could become the world's first mechanical whale. In most respects, it looks like an ordinary submarine. The difference is that in the bow is a huge "mouth" which would be mechanically opened when a school of krill is approached, then closed when the catch is taken inside.

Elsewhere, the most extensive plankton-research project was one begun by an Englishman, Sir Alister Hardy, in 1932, and continued by others since then at the Oceanographic Laboratory in Edinburgh, Scotland. Collecting plankton in the North Sea, the study has produced perhaps the most exhaustive records of plankton behavior ever put together by man. In a single year, a plankton-gathering ship operated by the laboratory gathered plankton for research by traveling 112,000 miles.

The data scientists receive from such research is not directly aimed at making plankton a food source for man. What interests them is the role this abundant sea life plays in the migration of fish. This helps commercial fishermen better understand the marine food chain. And this knowledge, in turn, increases the possibility not only of more efficiently exploiting fish stocks but in developing marine farms as well.

In recent years, a great variety of other edible sea animals and plants have been studied as possible sea-farmed food sources for man. The octopus and its close relative, the squid, for instance, are both harvested in Asian countries for human food, but their popularity has not yet gained a foothold in the Western world. Octopus and squid are sometimes served fresh; another means of preparing them is to dry them on racks placed in the sunshine. Although neither is sea farmed in the United States, there has been considerable discussion about doing so. The same is true of spiny sea urchins. Though they are considered a choice delicacy in Asia and are extensively sea farmed and harvested from the open sea as well, in the United States they are consid-

Squid, harvested in the Sea of Japan, are placed on racks to dry for market.

*Spiny sea urchin, predator of kelp*

ered more of a nuisance to swimmers and divers.

Members of the echinoderms, sea urchins are generally small, round, symmetrically shaped animals covered with prickly spines. If touched, the spines can produce a painful cut. Because of this, the spines are the urchin's main means of self-protection.

The meat inside the urchin, however, is quite tasty. In some parts of the world it is served as a topping in seafood cocktails. Since World War II, one small commercial company on the coast of Maine has harvested more than 75,000 pounds of urchins. Except in the research laboratory, however, the urchin in the United States has not created much interest except to this small company.

Finally, there is the abalone. A relative of the clams, oysters, squid, and octopi (all mollusks), this single-shelled animal is becoming one of the most extensively researched and farmed seafoods in many parts of the world.

If you have visited a seaside curio shop or gift shop, you have probably seen an abalone shell. Inlaid with many-colored, pearl-like bits of material, it is very popular as an ash tray or as a fruit bowl. The colorful shell is also made into jewelry.

It is in the meat of the abalone, however, that its real value lies. One of the ocean's most succulent dishes, it has often been called "the sirloin of the sea." It can, in fact, be served as a steak, and it has the tastiness of veal. Placed in a hot, buttered pan, abalone is cooked for only about thirty seconds on each side, then served immediately with lemon or cocktail sauce.

Abalone is excellent for dieters. It contains only about 1.01 calories per gram, has practically no fat, and is nearly 20 per cent protein. Studies have also shown that it is loaded with *antimicrobial* substances, that is, when eaten it is very effective in combating certain viruses. For these rea-

*Young abalone*

sons, the abalone has traditionally been a delicacy widely hunted by divers. The greatest abalone populations are found in Australia, on the west coast of North America, and in South and West Africa and the Canary Islands.

The abalones' living habits make it easy for divers to harvest them. Soon after they are spawned (each adult female lays about 2 million eggs), the young animals move about for about two weeks as free-swimming larvae. Then they settle down on a hard, rocky surface and move very little the rest of their lives. From this point to market-size maturity requires as long as seven years.

After choosing a rock for their home, they clamp themselves tightly to it by means of a thick muscle, and feed on minute algae that drift by. To harvest abalones, divers carry a heavy metal implement; great strength must be exerted to pry the adult abalone from its rocky home.

Over the years, particularly in California, overharvesting

*Abalone farming at Turtle Bay, Baja California, Mexico*

*Harvested abalone returned to dock for processing and canning.*

of this succulent animal threatened to wipe out the entire population. In addition to passing laws to limit the number of them taken, many states and countries, about ten years ago, launched extensive research programs in an effort to increase the dwindling number.

In one such program, 10,000 seedling abalones, hatched at a commercial sea farm in northern California, were transplanted to a bay in Mexico nearly 1,000 miles away. The purpose was to determine whether young abalones could survive the shock of transplantation, so that similar work could be conducted elsewhere.

To reduce the chance of shock, the young abalones were flown in a high-speed aircraft from San Francisco in California to the community of Bahia Tortugas in Baja California, Mexico.

Bahia Tortugas (Turtle Bay) is a community of about 3,000 people, most of whom earn their living diving for abalone in nearby bays and inlets. Upon their arrival in Mexico, the young abalones were taken into the sea by these divers and hand-planted on rocks which, it was hoped, would be chosen for the future homes. Screens of very fine wire mesh were then placed over the transplanted animals to protect them from fish predators.

Some of the transplanted abalones died in the experiment, as sponsoring scientists expected they might. But many thousands of others survived. A year after the transplant took place, divers returned to the scene and found that the abalones had begun to mature.

The future livelihood of the citizens of Turtle Bay was thus given a healthy boost. And another experiment in the increasingly important business of sea farming had proved successful.

Chapter **8**

# Tomorrow's Sea Farm

The sea is an enormous life-sustaining resource. It was only recently, as earth history is measured, that man began to tap this great storehouse on a major scale. Now that the vast amounts of potential food in the world seas is better known and understood, man has increasingly turned from sea hunter to sea farmer. He has done this with the able assistance of scientists and technicians, and the adventurous spirit of those who dive in the sea for sport or for a living.

Farming the edge of the sea, though still limited, is now a reality. On tomorrow's sea farm, man will go deeper to plant and harvest his "wet crops," and he will remain below longer. That deep-sea farm will be a wondrous place to behold.

Based on present-day predictions and existing technology, sea farmers will actually build "ranch houses" in the sea. They will employ small maneuverable submarines to move about. Quite possibly, man's warm-blooded mammal cousins in the sea—the dolphins, sea lions, and whales—will join him as "cowboys" of a sort. And from the world of technology will come a host of scientific aids to help him till and reap his underwater crops.

In the nineteenth century, a famous science-fiction

*Under construction in Japan: Aquapolis, the world's first floating city. Built for the 1975 International Ocean Exposition on the island of Okinawa, it is a prototype of future cities in the sea which may be built to service tomorrow's underwater farms.*

writer, Jules Verne, wrote a book called *Twenty Thousand Leagues Under the Sea*. Purely fiction, it described how man traveled deep in the sea in spacious submarines, encountering huge sea monsters and admiring the great beauty of the underwater world.

Verne's book was enormously popular at the time, probably because man had not yet developed the technology and skill of venturing far into the deep ocean. Now he has.

Although no monsters like those Verne described have been encountered, generations of human divers have found that Verne's dreams of great deep-sea beauty are entirely true. And at last they have also recognized that man can live and work in the ocean as he lives and works on the land.

In 1964, two men spent 49 hours living in a huge rubberized capsule, nicknamed SPID (for submersible portable inflatable dwelling) at a depth of 432 feet near the Bahama Islands in the Atlantic Ocean. One of the men was an American, Jon Lindbergh. The other was a Belgian, Robert Stenuit. Their project set records at the time, both for depth and endurance.

There have been many experiments in living-in-the-sea since then, and the knowledge gained may quite possibly lead to the building of full-scale "ranch houses" in the deep. The United States Navy conducted two important underwater-living experiments called SeaLab I and II. To remain in the deep sea, scientists have developed a technique called *saturation diving*. Unlike divers who carry their own air supply to and from the surface, and are thus limited in deep-sea time, saturation diving allows humans

*Habitat used in SeaLab I experiment*

*A drawing of the Navy's SeaLab III, showing how a support ship on the surface supplies electrical power and other necessities to a crew below. The same concept may be used for extracting oceanic mineral resources and underwater crops in the future.*

to remain below almost indefinitely.

Saturation diving involves a complicated scientific formula. Greatly simplified, it means that once body tissues are "saturated" with the gas breathed at any depth, and as long as the pressure inside an undersea station such as SPID equals the pressure outside, a diver can move in and out freely. And on his return to the surface, the time required to free him of the absorbed gases through decompression remains the same—no matter how long he stays down. Development of the saturation technique eliminated time spent below as a factor in computing how long the diver must decompress—only the depth at which he had remained.

With the development of habitats that allow men to remain in the sea for long periods have come a number of other aids for the future sea farmer. Here are just a few examples:

• *Submersibles*—For performing both shallow and deep-sea tasks, marine engineers have designed a number of small service people-carriers. They operate on the same principle as large military submarines, but are used primarily for research work and the development of marine resources. On some of the smallest, the operator is not enclosed within the vehicle, but sits in an open water "cockpit," wearing a scuba diving outfit.

Submersibles have been used in some sea-farming projects, although this capability has not gone beyond the experimental stage. Although not a crop in the food sense, some kinds of precious corals used for jewelry and decorative purposes have been successfully "harvested" by submersibles in Hawaii.

• *Electronic "corrals"*—How can fish be kept from straying underwater? In various experiments, scientists have developed "fences" that do the job well. One type consists of hollow pipe laid on the sea floor; air pumped into the pipe escapes through tiny holes in the pipe and rises to the surface. Scientists have found that although the bubbles do not harm them, fish will not swim through the bubbly fence and may be easily "corraled" in this manner. Bubble curtains have been successfully used to trap schools of herring on the coast of Maine.

In another project, marine scientists have experimented with different kinds of sounds sent out by underwater transmitters, and with instruments that transmit mild electric currents. Although both sound and electrical current are invisible, the scientists discovered that fish can be effectively controlled by using them.

• *Mammal "cowboys"*—Anyone who has visited an oceanarium knows how friendly and inventive the air-breathing porpoise can be. Nearly as intelligent as man himself, porpoises have assisted man in various underwater tasks. A porpoise named Tuffy, for instance, served as a messenger and tool carrier between the surface and an underwater habitat during one of the Navy's SeaLab experiments. Scientists envision how porpoises might serve on tomorrow's sea farms in a similar manner. Although they are fisheaters themselves, they can be trained to "herd" fish underwater at man's command and thus would function very much like cowboys on the land.

The porpoise is not the only potential mammal farmhand. In a series of experiments off the California coast, scientists of the U.S Naval Undersea Center successfully trained both sea lions and killer whales to do similar work. Sea lions retrieved costly torpedoes and missiles lying on the sea floor. And a killer whale named Ahab retrieved objects as deep as 1,500 feet. Although sea mammals doubtless will continue to assist man, new federal laws are designed to prevent their overexploitation.

*An artist's concept of an underwater sea farm of tomorrow. While diver-farmers till the wet sea floor, aided by dolphins, corralled fish are kept in pens by bubble fences. The habitat represents the underwater ranch house.*

- *Television*—One of the problems of working in the sea is that humans on the surface cannot see what is going on below. To overcome this obstacle, television is being used increasingly to give man "eyes" in the depths without having to dive there himself. Many of the deep-diving submersibles are equipped with pressurized TV cameras so that surface crews can view the underwater world as well as those in the vehicles themselves.

Television is helping, too, in scientific experiments designed to acquire new knowledge about marine resources. In one such project, a highly sensitive TV camera—similar to one used on Apollo moon flights—was used by the National Marine Fisheries Service.

The camera was placed in an aircraft which flew at night at 6,000 feet above the Gulf of Mexico and off the California coast. Although it was dark, sections of the sea below are dimly lighted by the faint glow of bioluminescence of swarms of plankton. In the sea, many marine animals emit a light, the same as the firefly does in the atmosphere of the dry continents.

The scientists knew that many species of fish feed on plankton. By locating the biggest areas of plankton with their TV cameras, they could in turn determine the location of schools of fish nearby. This information was then radioed to commercial fishing boats in the area, which moved in for the harvest.

These are only a few of the areas that scientists and technicians are exploring as possible aids for sea farming of tomorrow. Meanwhile, they are continuing to study and develop the more conventional crops—the fish, lobsters, oysters, and seaweed that are found in great numbers in shallow waters close to the coasts.

Certainly, it will not be a single sea crop or a single farming technique that will ultimately provide man with the vast amounts of new seafood he will require in the future. Success will depend upon a combination of crops and scientific efforts. Today, man is working steadily in this direction.

Most important, he is determining the degree to which various forms of pollution are affecting sea crops, and how these crop-destroying substances may best be controlled or eliminated.

Should he lose the scientific battle against pollution, man will never develop his full potential as a sea farmer. The effect of pollution was never better demonstrated than in what happened in Japan during several critical months of 1973. Residents of an island nation, the Japanese depend heavily upon the sea as a source of food; nearly 23 per cent of the protein for that country's 105 million people comes from fish alone. The Japanese eat fish baked, broiled, fried, salted, and even raw. Fishing is a huge industry in this Asian country, and an important part of the national economy.

In 1973, Japanese fisheries biologists discovered to their dismay that various forms of pollution, from a number of sources, had affected fishing so adversely that most seafood brought in for processing was too contaminated for human consumption.

Fish canneries closed, throwing thousands of Japanese out of work. Fishing boats remained idle in port. Realizing that the problem was a major one, the Japanese government set aside huge sums of money to determine the sources of pollution. It passed laws to control the many offenders: industrial plants discharging wastes into once-clean waterways, for instance.

Gradually, Japan's important coastal waters began improving in quality and the fishing industry eventually recovered. To a lesser degree, other nations have faced the same problem. And they have determined that man's carelessness in the form of pollution can easily wipe out his many gains in reaping the bountiful harvest of the ocean.

As long as man keeps this lesson in mind, he doubtless will even more fully farm the sea for the benefit of all humans on earth.

# Index

*Page numbers in* **boldface** *type indicate illustrations*

Abalone, 21, 24, 75, 80-84
Algae, 38, 39, 62, 69, 70, 72, 82
Algin, 70, 73
*Amanari,* 70
*Amas,* **64,** 65
Anchovy, 23
Aquaculture, definition of, 10
Aquapolis, **86,**
Arthropods, 46

Bait fish, 26
Bass
 kelp, 43
 sand, 43
Breeding, 23, 30, 31, 49

California Institute of Technology, 74
Calimar, Inc., 51
Carlisle, John G., 43
Carlsbad, California, 18
Carp, 30, 31
Carrageenan, 72
Catfish, 24, **28,** 29
Chickens, 30
Clam chowder, 66
Clams, 56, 63, 65-66, **66**
Commercial Fisheries, U. S. Bureau of, 26
Copepods, 50
Coral, 89
Coral reefs, 38-39
Cormorants, **11**
"Corrals," electronic, 89-90, **91**
"Cowboys," mammal, 90
Crabs, 46, 55
Crayfish, spiny, 44

Crossbreeding, *see* Breeding
Crustaceans, 46-55, 77

Diving, saturation, 87, 89
Dolphin, 85, **91**
Domsea Farms, **16, 17,** 17-18, **21,** 21, 25
Dulse, 72

Echinoderms, 81

Fish, **8,** 13, 14, 23-37, 75, 92
 bait, 26
 migration of, 78
Fish flour, 35, 36
Fish meal, 26
Fish protein concentrate (FPC), 35-36
Food chain, 37, 78
Fujinaga, Dr. Motosaku, 49, 50

Gesner, Konrad von, 31
Groupers, 23
Gumbo, 47
*Gyosho,* 44

Hake, 36
Halibut, 34, 43
*Hamachi,* 27
Hardy, Sir Alister, 78
Hawaii Fish and Game Division, 41
Herring, 23, 90
Holdfasts, 71, 75

Irish moss, 72-73

Kelp, **8**, 43, 69, 70, 73-75
*Koi*, 31
Krill, 77

*Limu*, 72
Lindbergh, Jon, 87
*Liquamen*, 35-36
Lobsters, **8**, 18, 45, 46, **52**, 52-55, 77, 92

Mackerel, **11**, 26
Maraculture, 10
Marifarm, 50
Marine protein concentrate (MPC), 35
Metamorphosis, 34
Mexico, Gulf of, 18, 39, 47, 60, 92
Milkfish, 15, 31, 32-33
Mollusks, 46, 56-68
Molting, 46
Mullet, 29-30
Mussels, 15, 56, 63, 65, 66-67, **67**

National Marine Fisheries Service, 26, 36, 92
Navy, U. S., 17-18
*Nori*, 70-71

Oceanic Institute (Hawaii), 29
Octopus, 56, 78
Opaleye, 43
Overfishing, 27, 37, 63
Oyster drill, 59
Oysters, **8**, 14, 15, **19**, 19-20, 21, 56-65, 92

Paradise Cove (California), 42-43
Pearls, 63-65
Perch, surf, **41**, 43
Photosynthesis, 71
Plaice, 33-35
Plankton, 26, 50, 69, 76-78, 92
Plants, 69-75
Pliny, 35
Pollution, 20, 22, 25, 27, 34, 37, 45, 60, 63, 93-94
  thermal, 62
Pompano, 27
Porpoise, 90
Prawns, **25**

Ray, Dr. Sammy, 18-20
Rays, 23
  electric, 43
Reefs
  artificial, 38-45
  coral, 38-39

Regeneration, 55
Rockfish, 43

Salmon, **16**, 17, **17**, 18, **21**, 21, 25, 30, 31-32
San Diego Gas & Electric Company, 18
Sand dabs, 43
*Sapona* (freighter), 38, 39
Sardines, 23, 26
Sargo, 43
Saturation diving, 87, 89
Scallops, 56, 63, 65, 67-68
Schlesser, Dr. Robert, 54
Schumann, Dr. George, 26
Scripps Institution of Oceanography, 43-44
Sea cucumber, 44
Sea Grant Program, 18, 21, 22, 74, 75
Sea lions, 85, 90
Sea urchins, 44, 75, 78, 80
SeaLab, 87, **87**, **88**, 90
Seaweed, **8**, 14, 21, 69-72, 92
Sharks, 23
Sheepshead, 42, 43
Shellbourne, Dr. James, 33-35
Shellfish, 14, 24, 46
Shrimp, **8**, 21, 22, 46-47, **47**, **48**, 49-52, 77
  brine, 26, 49, 50, 51
Spats, 59
Squid, 78, **79**
Starfish, 59, 62, 68
Stenuit, Robert, 87
Stereotropism, 39
Submersible portable inflatable dwelling (SPID), 87, 89
Submersibles, 89, 92

Takata, Michio, 41
Television, underwater use of, 92
*Tempura*, 47
Teredo borers, **44**
Tropism, 39
Trout, **12**, **14**, 30-31
*Tsukiiso*, 44

Urchins, *see* Sea urchins

Veligers, 57-58
Verne, Jules, 86-87

Whale, 85
  blue, 77
  killer, 90
Wilcox, Dr. Howard A., 75

96

61214

| DATE DUE | | | |
|---|---|---|---|
| SEP 2 7 1990 | | | |
| | | | |
| | | | |
| | | | |
| | | | |
| | | | |
| | | | |
| | | | |
| | | | |
| | | | |
| | | | |
| | | | |
| | | | |

639  Brown, Joseph E.
B    The sea's harvest.

DISCARDED

290096 04627A